The Star-Spangled Banner

By Francis Scott Key
Illustrated by Dana Regan

A Random House PICTUREBACK® Book
Random House 🏠 New York

Illustrations copyright © 2002 by Dana Regan. Sidebar text copyright © 2002 by Random House, Inc. All rights reserved under International and Pan-American Copyright Conventions. Published in the United States by Random House, Inc., New York, and simultaneously in Canada by Random House of Canada Limited, Toronto.
www.randomhouse.com/kids
Library of Congress Cataloging-in-Publication Data
Key, Francis Scott, 1779–1843.   The star-spangled banner / song by Francis Scott Key ; illustrated by Dana Regan.
— 1st ed.   p.   cm. — (A Random House picture back book)   SUMMARY: Lyrics to the United States national anthem are accompanied by illustrations and text about national monuments, holidays, and moments in American history.
ISBN 0-375-81596-1 (trade) —   ISBN 0-375-91596-6 (lib. bdg.)
1. Star-spangled banner (Song)—Juvenile literature. 2. United States—Songs and music. 3. National songs—United States—Texts.
[1. Star-spangled banner (Song). 2. United States—Songs and music. 3. National songs—United States.]
I. Regan, Dana, ill. II. Title. III. Series.   PZ8.3.K47 St 2002   782.42'1599'0973—dc21   [E]   2001048769
Printed in the United States of America   First Edition May 2002   10 9 8 7 6 5 4 3 2 1
PICTUREBACK, RANDOM HOUSE and colophon, and PLEASE READ TO ME and colophon are registered trademarks of Random House, Inc.

Oh, say, can you see, by the dawn's early light,
What so proudly we hailed at the twilight's last gleaming?

The American Flag

Betsy Ross sewed the first American flag in 1776. That flag had 13 stars and 13 stripes to symbolize the 13 original colonies. Today's flags still have 13 stripes, but now they have 50 stars for the 50 states. The American flag is nicknamed "Old Glory" and "The Stars and Stripes."

Francis Scott Key

During the War of 1812, Francis Scott Key was watching as the British attacked Fort McHenry. When dawn came and our flag was still flying, he knew that the U.S. had won the battle. This inspired him to write "The Star-Spangled Banner," which became our national anthem in 1931.

September 14, 1814

Whose broad stripes and bright stars,
through the perilous fight,
O'er the ramparts we watched
were so gallantly streaming?

The Fourth of July

We celebrate July 4 as Independence Day because it was on that day, in 1776, that the Declaration of Independence was first signed. The first Independence Day, however, was celebrated on July 8, 1776, in Philadelphia. The Declaration of Independence was read aloud and bells rang in the streets.

And the rockets' red glare, the bombs bursting in air,
Gave proof through the night that our flag was still there.

Oh, say, does that star-spangled banner yet wave
O'er the land of the free and the home of the brave

Presidents
DID YOU KNOW?

★ John and Abigail Adams became the first President and First Lady to move into the White House, in 1800.

★ Abraham Lincoln was the tallest President at 6'4". James Madison was the shortest at 5'4".

★ The teddy bear was named after President Theodore "Teddy" Roosevelt.

★ The President's office is called the Oval Office.

On the shore dimly seen
through the mists of the deep,
Where the foe's haughty host
in dread silence reposes,

What is that which the breeze,
o'er the towering steep,
As it fitfully blows,
half conceals, half discloses?

Westward Ho!

American pioneers went west for many reasons. Some were looking for land to farm. Some were looking for jobs on the railroad or in lumber camps. Some even went to Colorado and California looking for gold! The one thing they all had in common was that they were looking for a new life on the American frontier.

Now it catches the gleam
of the morning's first beam,

In full glory reflected,
now shines on the stream;

Wagon Trains

Before the railroad went all the way to California, people moved west in covered wagons. For protection, settlers traveled in groups called wagon trains. At night, they would circle the wagons around the campfire for warmth and to make it easier to keep watch for danger.

The Bald Eagle
DID YOU KNOW?

★ The bald eagle is the official national bird of the U.S.

★ It was chosen by Congress on June 20, 1782.

★ It represents freedom, strength, and majesty.

★ Ben Franklin wanted the turkey to be our national bird, but the bald eagle won out.

'Tis the star-spangled banner: oh, long may it wave

O'er the land of the free
and the home of the brave!

Mount Rushmore

The busts of George Washington, Thomas Jefferson, Theodore Roosevelt, and Abraham Lincoln make up the sculpture we know as Mount Rushmore. These heads are the largest stone sculptures in the world. They average 60 feet high. That's six stories! The sculpture, begun in 1927, took 14 years and one million dollars to build!

State Facts
DID YOU KNOW?

★ The last two states to be added to the U.S. were Alaska and Hawaii in 1959. These states are not connected to the other 48.

★ Delaware was the first to ratify the Constitution and officially become a state.

★ The smallest state in area is Rhode Island. The biggest in area is Alaska.

And where is that band who so vauntingly swore
That the havoc of war and the battle's confusion
A home and a country should leave us no more?

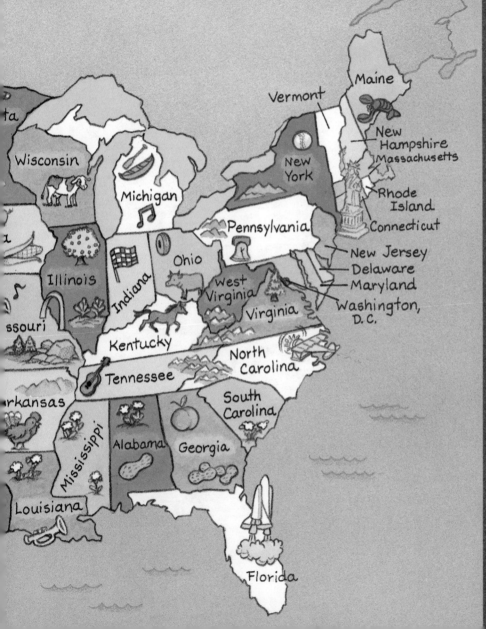

Their blood has washed out their foul footsteps' pollution.
No refuge could save the hireling and slave
From the terror of flight or the gloom of the grave,

And the star-spangled banner
in triumph doth wave
O'er the land of the free
and the home of the brave.

Oh, thus be it ever when free men shall stand,
Between their loved homes and the war's desolation;
Blessed with victory and peace, may the heaven-rescued land
Praise the Power that has made and preserved us as a nation!

Martin Luther King, Jr.

Martin Luther King, Jr., believed all people are created equal. He worked hard for the cause of civil rights and equality in the 1950s and 1960s. He gave his famous "I Have a Dream" speech from the steps of the Lincoln Memorial in Washington, D.C., on August 28, 1963. About 250,000 people came to listen.

We shall Overcome

Then conquer we must, when our cause is just,
And this be our motto: "In God is our trust";

And the star-spangled banner in triumph shall wave
O'er the land of the free and the home of the brave!